GuitarQuotes

Inspiration from the World's
Best Players

D. A. Ogren

GuitarQuotes

GuitarQuotes: Inspiration from the World's Best Players

"Guitar" Image (Practicing Chapter) courtesy of Daniel St.Pierre at FreeDigitalPhotos.net
"Electric Guitar" Image (Playing Chapter) courtesy of dan at FreeDigitalPhotos.net
"Guitar" Image (Players Chapter) courtesy of Dino De Luca at FreeDigitalPhotos.net
"Guitar Knobs" Image (Passion Chapter) courtesy of coward lion at FreeDigitalPhotos.net
"Hand In Rock N Roll Sign With Guitarist" Image (Personalities Chapter) courtesy of grandfailure at FreeDigitalPhotos.net
"Guitarist Of A Pop Band" Image (Performance Chapter) courtesy of phanlop88 at FreeDigitalPhotos.net
"Music Icon Set" Image (electric guitar on each page) courtesy of digitalart at FreeDigitalPhotos.net
"Music Icon" Image (acoustic guitar on each page) courtesy of zirconicusso at FreeDigitalPhotos.net

...other books by D. A. Ogren

Acoustic Guitar Care 101: A Survival Guide for Beginners

The Last Bucket List: Think Big. Be Changed. Give Life

Adventurous RV: the Ultimate Logbook for those Charting their Own Course

Market to Millions: The Ultimate Directory to Free eBook Promotion

Table of Contents

Introduction

From that simple season of youth, we aimed to emulate our favorite players: the axe-slaying metal-heads with their scorching solos and core-jarring power chords; the nimble, arpeggio-driven classicists that stirred the mind and emotions with sounds both exotic and ancient; the cool-cat jazz musicians noodling on guitars the size of a truck, making us dream of urban clubs and noir nightlife; the comfort-food warmth of the acoustic sojourner, calling us to alternate tunings and new visions, and removing past boundaries of the guitar's capabilities.

Guitar music, and the players that inspire it, follows us through life, reminding us of the past, creating new experiences, and building a context for the ebb and flow of life. The innumerable tonalities, emotions and expressions that guitars and guitarists evoke never cease to astound, move and challenge us. With that in mind, the quotes of our beloved guitarists have particular importance and weight, providing a window into their thoughts and motivations, struggles and joys. Further, their sayings impart wisdom, for both novice and experienced players, by teaching how to practice, improve stage presence, select guitars, and how to truly celebrate the guitar.

I hope you enjoy these quotes as much as I have, and that, no matter what style you prefer, you will perhaps find a new love and a greater appreciation for the vast world that is guitar playing, guitar music and guitar players.

— DAVID OGREN

Playing

GuitarQuotes

I believe every guitar player inherently has something unique about their playing. They just have to identify what makes them different and develop it.

— JIMMY PAGE

Playing guitar is not a beauty contest.

— ERNIE ISLEY

Finding ways to use the same guitar people have been using for 50 years to make sounds that no one has heard before is truly what gets me off.

— JEFF BECK

If you pick up a guitar and it says 'Take me, I'm yours,' then that's the one for you.

— FRANK ZAPPA

"Whenever I get down on my playing, I just bend a note, shake it and listen. What I hear sound so great it makes me realize that even a rut doesn't suck."

— DIMEBAG DARRELL

A good player can make any guitar sound good.

— MICHAEL BLOOMFIELD

When you play the guitar, you don't have to say nothing. The girls would say something to you.

– BUDDY GUY

Let me explain something about guitar playing…Everyone's approach to what can come out of six strings is different from another person, but it's all valid.

- JIMMY PAGE

We don't want any vocalist messing up the music.

- JOHN SCOFIELD

You don't find a style. It finds you.

— KEITH RICHARDS

As long as you're excited about what you're playing, and as long as it comes from your heart, it's going to be great.

— JOHN FRUSCIANTE

Playing the guitar is like telling the truth.

— B.B. KING

...play every day and take it in front of other people. They need to hear it and you need them to hear it.

— JAMES TAYLOR

So, my big brother was playing guitar and I figured I'd try it too.

- STEVIE RAY VAUGHAN

I was 16 when I started playing. I borrowed a friend's acoustic guitar, and I had a Beatles chord book. I just taught myself that way.

- BRITT DANIEL

I don't understand why some people
will only accept a guitar if it has an
instantly recognizable guitar sound.

— JEFF BECK

If you play acoustic guitar you are the
depressed, sensitive guy.

— ELLIOTT SMITH

I've always thought that the act of
playing the guitar was the act of trying
to make a point of playing the guitar.

— MICK RONSON

Most people are trying to figure out 'how do I get in the fast lane going that way?'. I'm going in the other direction. I wanna find the oldest thing to do.

– ERIC CLAPTON

If you pick up a guitar and it say 'Take me, I'm yours,' then that's the one for you.

— *FRANK ZAPPA*

If you don't know the blues... there's no point in picking up the guitar and playing rock and roll or any other form of popular music.

— *KEITH RICHARDS*

I'd much rather talk about guitar playing. I hate it when people ask mem about my lyrics.

— *JAMES HETFIELD*

Playing guitar was one of my childhood hobbies, and I had played a little at school and at camp…but it was a hobby – nothing more.

– BONNY RAITT

I lie around and play guitar, that's something I do for sure. In fact that's all I do, I think.

– EVAN DANDO

To me, the guitar is a tool for songwriting, and it's fun, too. The day that it's not fun, that's when I'm not gonna play guitar anymore

– SCOTT IAN

I think it's important to learn how to
play the guitar. To play music is one of
the greatest things.

— *PRINCE*

The guitar is an orchestra.

— *LUDWIG VAN BEETHOVEN*

I learned to play guitar at a young age
and converted poems and stuff that I
had written to songs.

— *GREGORY HARRISON*

Without question Gibson guitars are the finest, most revered guitars on the planet.

— TED NUGENT

I approach playing acoustic guitar more of as a percussive instrument. It's fragile. I don't have a lot of finesse when it comes to my guitar playing.

— BILLIE JOE ARMSTRONG

Guitar playing is both extremely easy for me and extremely difficult for me at the same time.

— KIRK HAMMETT

I don't play a lot of fancy guitar. I don't want to play it. The kind of guitar I want to play is mean, mean licks.

— JOHN LEE HOOKER

With a guitar I would be able to express the things I felt in sounds.

— WILLIAM CHRISTOPHER HANDY

As a guitar player, you can gravitate to the blues because you can play it easily... It's purely emotive and dead easy to get a start with.

— BOZ SCAGGS

If you have a great-sounding guitar that's a quality instrument…that's the key. It starts with the guitar and knowing what it should sound and feel like.

— EDDIE VAN HALEN

I've been imitated so well I've heard people copy my mistakes.

— JIMI HENDRIX

When all the original blues guys are gone, you start to realize that someone has to tend to the tradition. I recognize that I have some responsibility to keep the music alive, and it's a pretty honorable position to be in.

— ERIC CLAPTON

When you play the 12-string guitar, you
spend half your life tuning the
instrument and the other half playing it
out of tune.

— *PETE SEEGER*

I never stop being amazed by all the
different ways of playing the guitar and
making it deliver a message.

— *LES PAUL*

In jazz improv, there is no such thing as
wrong notes, only notes that are better
chosen and it's not about the note you
play, it's about the note you play next.

— *LARRY CARLTON*

I still play that guitar. It's a Martin D-18 with a clear pick guard. I've played that guitar on and off my TV shows for nearly 50 years.

— ANDY GRIFFITH

I get to play a scorching lead guitar, and there's not much that's more fun than that.

— PETER TORK

I got my first guitar when I was 15, and I just used to fool about with it, more or less, as time went by, though, I got more interested.

— PAUL McCARTNEY

…when I did finally get the guitar, it didn't seem that difficult to me, to be able to make a good noise out of it.

— ERIC CLAPTON

Nobody seems to play Yamaha electrics, but it's the best guitar I own.

— SCOTT PUTESKY

There's so much that can be done on the guitar…everyone can really enjoy themselves on it and have a good time, which is what it's all about.

— JIMMY PAGE

The heavy guitars are the ones that sound good. They are not that comfortable, but they do sound great.

— NEAL SCHON

It all comes down to the density of the wood. Every guitar's different.

— ROBIN TROWER

My dad was vehemently opposed to electric guitars. He did not look on that kind of music as legitimate in any way.

— DAN FOGELBERG

My older sister encouraged me from early on and bought me one of the first guitars I had. She listened to all of the crappy songs that I wrote...

— TRACY CHAPMAN

Rock & Roll is feeling, and after you know most of the basics...getting that feeling is just about the most important aspect of playing guitar.

— *EDDIE VAN HALEN*

A good player can make any guitar sound good.

— *MIKE BLOOMFIELD*

When I started to play with my fingernails, it was not just for volume. The most important thing was giving the guitar different colors in its voices...

— *ADRES SEGOVIA*

I find it to be an ongoing challenge to keep the guitar from becoming too traditional.

— EDGE

Your sound is in your hands as much as anything. It's the way you pick, and the way you hold the guitar, more than it is the amp or the guitar you use.

— STEVIE RAY VAUGHAN

Guitarists should be able to pick up the guitar and play music on it for an hour, without a rhythm section or anything.

— JOE PASS

I can embarrass myself very easily on guitar. It's funny because people say to me I can play anything…But I could make a big list of everything I can't play…

— JOE SATRIANI

Each guitar has its own character and personality, which can be magnified once the player engages in beatin' it up.

— BILLY GIBBONS

The stainless-steel frets were a major breakthrough…I have to get my guitars refretted every couple of months.

— EDDIE VAN HALEN

I got my first guitar at age of 7 and never laid it down. Momma taught me G, C, and D. I was off to the races son!

—JERRY REED

Playing guitar is a never-finished journey.

—JOHN FOGERTY

I wasn't put on this earth to amass money or personal wealth. I was put on this earth to play guitar and write songs.

— NOEL GALLAGHER

A guitar is just theoretically built wrong. Each string is an interval of fourths, and then the B string is off.

— *EDDIE VAN HALEN*

But the guitar, my lady, whether well played or badly played, well strung or badly strung, is pleasant to hear and listen to; being so easy to learn, it attracts the busiest of talented people and makes them put aside loftier occupations so that they may hold a guitar in their hands.

— *LUIS DE BRICENO*

Practicing

GuitarQuotes

I never practice my guitar…from time to time I just open the case and throw in a piece of raw meat.

— WES MONTGOMERY

Technique is paramount to the beginner. Only thoughtful, regular, and yes, joyful daily practice will enable the student of the guitar to develop mind muscles and spirit into a concord of execution and expression.

— AARON SHEARER

My best songs come from making a lot of mistakes and playing a lot of garbage.

— ERIC JOHNSON

I practice all the scales. Everyone should know lots of scales. Actually, I feel there are only scales. What is a chord, if not the notes of a scale hooked together?

—JOHN McLAUGHLIN

The beautiful thing about learning is that no one can take it away from you.

— B.B. KING

Most beginners want to learn lead because they think it's cool…learning lead should come after you can play solid backup and have the sound of the chords in your head.

— EDDIE VAN HALEN

Sometimes you want to give up the guitar, you'll hate the guitar. But if you stick with it, you're gonna be rewarded.

– JIMI HENDRIX

If you make the same mistake 3 times, that becomes 'your arrangment'.

– JORMA K.

I just play, just you know, if I just sit down with the guitar and just do whatever for, you know, a half hour or an hour or whatever. That's pretty much, that should do it for me.

– SLASH

If you really love guitar, you're going to spend every waking hour stroking the thing.

— FRANK ZAPPA

If you want music to be your livelihood, then play, play, play and play! And eventually, you'll get to where you want to be.

— EDDIE VAN HALEN

I have only one teacher, myself, and only one student, myself.

— ANDRES SEGOVIA

One day you pick up the guitar and you feel like a great master, and the next day you feel like a fool. It's because we're different every day, but the guitar is always the same…beautiful.

— *TOMMY EMMANUEL*

I wasn't invited to parties and I look back now and I'm so thankful that I was at home, playing the guitar until my fingers bled.

— TAYLOR SWIFT

I dedicated all the time I had to it. The 10 hour workout was just what I put in the magazine at the time, but for me it was every waking moment.

— STEVE VAI

When I got my first guitar my fingers wouldn't go to the sixth string so I took off the big E and played with just five strings. I was only 6 or 7.

— LES PAUL

I could care less about sitting around
and practicing the guitar for hours a day
and trying to be the best guitar player on
the planet.

— SCOTT IAN

Listening is the key to everything good
in music.

— PAT METHENY

The guitar has always been abused with
distortion units and funny sorts of
effects, but when you don't do that and
just let the genuine sound come through,
there's a whole magic there.

—JEFF BECK

I don't read music. I don't write it. So I wander around on the guitar until something starts to present itself.

—JAMES TAYLOR

I'm retired now so the practice is down to just 4 hours.

—JULIAN BREAM

Any guitar solo should reflect the music that it's soloing over and not just be existing in its own sort of little world.

— JOHN FRUSCIANTE

I don't like to practice; I like spontaneity. When I don't play guitar for a week and I pick it up again, I play better.

— ACE FREHLEY

I try to practice like a well-rounded regiment of things…and I also have to practice the actual songs to keep that under my fingers as well.

— JOHN PETRUCCI

If you don't know the blues… there's no point in picking up the guitar and playing rock and roll or any other form of popular music.

— KEITH RICHARDS

It's not about how long you've been playing, it's about how long you play. Like I've been playing for 45 years, but when I was 18 I played more than I have done in the rest of my life.

– PHIL X

We all have idols. Play like anyone you care about but try to be yourself while you're doing so.

— B.B. KING

Learning to play the guitar is a combination of mental and motor skill acquisition. And to develop motor skill, repetition is essential.

— HOWARD ROBERTS

To stay a great singer or guitar player, you've got to do it 24/7. That's what I do.

— SAMMY HAGAR

I learned to tune a guitar by ear. That method has served me pretty well.

— CHARLEY PRIDE

Then when you find a cat that's really playing, you always find that he's been playing a long time, you can't get around it.

— WES MONTGOMERY

If someone can relate my guitar solo to an exercise in a book... that's no fun at all.

—JOE SATRIANI

Sometimes, you don't need a $5,000 guitar - you need $5,000 worth of lessons.

— CHRIS SMITHER

Approach your guitar intelligently…Somethings you can do better than others, some things you can't do as well. So accentuate the positive.

— CHET ATKINS

As far as guitar goes, it's weird to have such a challenging activity in my life for so long - I love it. It kicks my ass every day.

— VERNON REID

I'm like a bad musical cliche because I bring my guitar on the road and try to write songs in hotel rooms.

— MOBY

One must make of one's fingers well drilled soldiers.

— FERNANDO SOR

When you tune your guitar in a different way, it lends itself to a new way of looking at your songwriting.

— SHERYL CROW

If I don't practice one day, I know it; two days, the critics know it; three days, the public knows it.

— JASCHA HEIFETZ

Regardless of what you play, the biggest thing is keeping the feel going.

— WES MONTGOMERY

My guitar taught me to sing in textures, from the roundest lingering harmonic to the sharpest snap of a pulled string.

— ANI DiFRANCO

A different guitar will have different strengths and weaknesses. If you learn how different guitars want to be touched, you have a wider repertoire of tonal technique on all guitars. My guitars were frequently my teachers.

– David Bromberg

Passion

GuitarQuotes

My guitar is not a thing. It is an
extension of myself. It is who I am.

—JOAN JETT

A guitar is a very personal extension of
the person playing it. You have to be
emotionally and spiritually connected to
your instrument.

— EDDIE VAN HALEN

To me a guitar is kind of like a
woman. You don't know why you like
'em but you do.

— WAYLON JENNINGS

The time I burned my guitar it was like a
sacrifice. You sacrifice the things you
love. I love my guitar.

— JIMI HENDRIX

You take up the guitar in the first place
because you're an inarticulate person
and then you go out and talk eight hours
a day about it.

— WARREN ZEVON

I play guitar because it lets me dream
out loud.

— MICHAEL HEDGES

Sometimes the nicest thing to do with a guitar is just look at it.

— THOM YORKE

No matter where or what audience will watch you playing, get rid of judgments…play with passion and stream your truth.

— DALLTON SANTOS

One good thing about music, when it hits you, you feel no pain.

— BOB MARLEY

My first love was the sound of guitar.

—BOZ SCAGGS

Music doesn't lie. If there is something that needs to be changed in this world, then it can only happen through music.

—JIMI HENDRIX

It sounds hokey, but finding a focus on something - whether it's skateboard or playing your guitar - can be life changing.

— JEFF AMENT

I went to my friend's house one day, and he had an electric guitar he had just bought with a tiny little amp. I turned the volume up to 10 and I hit one chord, and I said, I'm in love.

— ACE FREHLEY

The guitar is a small orchestra. It is polyphonic. Every string is a different color, a different voice.

— ADRES SEGOVIA

It is the most delightful thing that ever happens to me, when I hear something coming out of my guitar and out of my mouth that wasn't there before.

— JAMES TAYLOR

Among God's creatures two, the dog and the guitar, have taken all the sizes and all the shapes, in order not to be separated from the man.

— Andres Segovia

A friend of mine…came up one day with an old guitar…he knew about two chords on it. He proceeded to teach them to me, and then we proceeded to go crazy over music.

— CHARLIE DANIELS

Besides being a guitar player, I'm a big fan of the guitar. I love that damn instrument.

— STEVE VAI

My guitar is like my best friend. My guitar can get me through anything…that's the greatest therapy for me.

— MILEY CYRUS

I always loved rock guitar…I had no aspirations to be a musician, but I picked up a guitar for two seconds and haven't put it down since.

— SLASH

Every time you pick up your guitar to play, play as if it's the last time.

— ERIC CLAPTON

…guitar is the perfect companion to the human voice. You rest it against your gut, against your heart, and when you strum it the vibrations go outwards for all to hear…

— JASON MRAZ

…the sound of an amplified guitar in a room full of people was so hypnotic and addictive to me, that I could cross any kind of border to get on there.

— ERIC CLAPTON

The guitar chose me.

— CHARLIE BYRD

Lean your body forward slightly to support the guitar against your chest, for the poetry of the music should resound in your heart.

— ANDRES SEGOVIA

When I pick up the guitar, it's a melody, and that's what drives the lyrics. It's bits and pieces of truth, but it is storytelling.

— RAY LaMONTAGNE

Music and rhythm find their way into the secret places of the soul.

— PLATO

There was a period when I'd just come out of college where I'd been playing classical guitar and I suddenly realized that it wasn't what I wanted to do with the rest of my life.

— ANDY SUMMERS

A guitar is like an old friend that is there with me.

— B.B. KING

I think it's so cool that you can pick up the guitar and create something that didn't exist 5 minutes ago…You have music at your fingertips.

— MICHELLE BRANCH

I'm only myself when I have a guitar in my hands.

— GEORGE HARRISON

That happens every time I get
behind a guitar, regardless of
what I'm saying, 'cause music
is freedom and being free is
the closest I've ever felt to
being spiritual.

— BEN HARPER

God is playing my guitar, I am with god
when I play.

— LINK WRAY

An uncle of mine emigrated to Canada
and couldn't take his guitar with him.
When I found it in the attic, I'd found a
friend for life.

— STING

The guitar was my weapon, my shield to
hide behind.

— BRIAN MAY

It was my love for the guitar that first got me into music and singing.

— ED SHEERAN

Guitars have been the obsession of my life. I first picked one up at the age of four and I've been a guitar junkie ever since.

— JOHNNY MARR

When I'm having a bad day, I pick up my guitar.

— MICHELLE BRANCH

My guitar was a loyal person to me.

— DAVE MUSTAINE

There are two kinds of music. One comes from the strings of a guitar, the other from the strings of the heart…That sweet sound of love.

— MICHAEL JACKSON

The most important part of my religion is to play guitar.

— LOU REED

I may not believe in myself, but I believe in what I'm doing.

—JIMMY PAGE

The guitar is a means of expressing music…Let me put it this way, Louis Armstrong once said if you've got to ask, you'll never know.

— CHARLIE BYRD

The guitar has a kind of grit and excitement possessed by nothing else.

— BRIAN MAY

Music is a necessity. After food, air, water and warmth, music is the next necessity of life.

— KEITH RICHARDS

With a guitar I would be able to express the things I felt in sounds.

— WILLIAM CHRISTOPHER HANDY

But the guitar, when you think about it, is the most versatile, really. I mean you can pick it up and take it with you wherever you go.

— ERIC CLAPTON

The guitar is a much more efficient machine than a computer. More responsive.

— COLIN GREENWOOD

Guitars have been the obsession of my life. I first picked one up at the age of four and I've been a guitar junkie ever since.

—JOHNNY MARR

Nothing is more beautiful than a guitar, except, possibly two.

— FREDERIC CHOPIN

My guitars are my umbilical cord.
They're directly wired into my head.

— KIRK HAMMETT

Whenever I find that I've got a problem,
I'll go pick my guitar up and play. It's
the greatest pal in the whole world.

— LES PAUL

If we replaced guns with guitars, then
the world would be a concert.

— THOMAS IAN NICHOLAS

I love the guitar for its harmony; it is my
constant companion in all my travels.

— NICCOLO PAGANINI

The [guitar is the] instrument most
complete and richest in its harmonic and
polyphonic possibilities.

— MANUEL DE FALLA

Technically, I'm not a guitar player, all I
play is truth and emotion.

— JIMI HENDRIX

The guitar is your first wings. It's assigned and designed to unfold your vision and imagination.

— CARLOS SANTANA

The guitar is a meditative tool to touch God and find love within yourself.

— PEPE ROMERO

I'm amazed that I can sit down, put a guitar in my hands and start playing kind of free style, and it will be four hours later and it will feel like it's been five minutes.

—JOHN RZEZNIK

I'm not trying to play the guitar. I'm trying to play music.

— MICHAEL HEDGES

The turning point in the history of western civilization was reached with the invention of the electric guitar.

— LENE SINCLAIR

A man can never have too many pairs of sunglasses or too many guitars.

— RICHIE SAMBORA

And if the world does turn, and if London burns, I'll be standing on the beach with my guitar.

— THOM YORKE

First guitars tend to be like first loves: ill-chosen, unsuitable, short-lived and unforgettable.

— TIM BROOKES

GuitarQuotes

Performance

GuitarQuotes

I want to figure out how I can make that most important statement with the least amount of information, so I don't run out of ideas by the time I get to my second or third chorus.

— LARRY CARLTON

I can communicate far better on a guitar, than I can through my mouth.

— JIMMY PAGE

Just as blues player can play 20 blues songs in a row but find a way to make each one different. I always want to find different ways to do something.

— JOE SATRIANI

Guitar is the best form of self-expression
I know. Everything else, and I'm just
sort of tripping around, trying to figure
my way through life.

— SLASH

I wanted to create music that was so
different that my mother could tell from
anyone else.

— LES PAUL

I'm pretty basic as far as technique is
concerned. I don't use many gadgets,
and I like the sound my guitar makes,
anyway.

— BRIAN MAY

If you've got a guitar and a lot of soul,
just bang something out and mean it.
You're the superstar.

— KRIST NOVOSELIC

I don't even know if I can take the credit
for writing 'Cliffs of Dover'. It was just
there for me one day, literally wrote in
five minutes, kind of a gift from a higher
place...

— ERIC JOHNSON

Guitar players never listen to lead
singers.

— STEVEN TYLER

To stand up on a stage alone
with an acoustic guitar
requires bravery bordering on
heroism. Bordering on
insanity.

– RICHARD THOMPSON

I'm pretty basic as far as technique is concerned. I don't use many gadgets, and I like the sound my guitar makes, anyway.

— BRIAN MAY

Anyone who used more than three chords is just showing off.

— WOODIE GUTHRIE

My vocation is more in composition really than anything else - building up harmonies using the guitar, orchestrating the guitar like an army, a guitar army.

—JIMMY PAGE

Every album, I'm worried that I'm a dork and a fraud…Then I stop thinking and start playing guitar, and I realize that it's okay to suck, and move forward.

— PINK

Someone told me the smile on my face gets bigger when I play the guitar.

— NIALL HORAN

As far as I'm concerned, I'm just a guitar player, and my job is to go out there and play and entertain and do my thing.

— LES PAUL

Notes and chords have become my second language and, more often than not, that vocabulary expresses what I feel when language fails me.

— SLASH

What I couldn't say verbally I was able to express physically through the guitar.

— DAVE MUSTAINE

I tried to connect my singing voice to my guitar an' my guitar to my singing voice. Like the two was talking to one another.

— B.B. KING

Arranging is the way I put my stamp on my music as much as my guitar playing.

— LEE RITENOUR

My guitar is a mutation between a classic Fender Stratocaster guitar, which I played for years, and a Gibson solid-body like an SG or a Les Paul...it does what I want it to do.

— JERRY GARCIA

Experimenting with different sounds is great, but when it comes down to it, you're still playing a guitar.

— SCOTT PUTESKY

I've looked at photographs of myself during concerts and it sometimes looks as if I'm in a fencing move, with a guitar in my hands instead of a sword.

— NEIL DIAMOND

When the intellectual part of guitar playing overrides the spiritual, you don't get to extreme heights.

—JOHN FRUSCIANTE

I didn't want to fall into the trap of competing with all these other great guitar players. I just want to sidestep the whole thing and get out of the race.

— KIRK HAMMETT

When I plug in my guitar and play it really loud, loud enough to deafen most people, that's my shot of adrenaline, and there's nothing like it.

−JOE PERRY

The more guitars we have onstage the better, as I'm concerned.

− BRUCE DICKINSON

Rock and Roll is simply an attitude. You don't have to play the greatest guitar.

−JOHNNY THUNDERS

Try to express your own ideas. It's much more difficult to do, but the rewards are there if you're good enough to pull it off.

— CHET ATKINS

Actually, because I'm so small, when I strike an open A chord I get physically thrown to the left, and when I play an open G chord I go right...I just go where the guitar takes me.

— ANGUS YOUNG

GuitarQuotes

Personalities

GuitarQuotes

I wish they'd had electric guitars in the cotton fields back in the good old days. A whole lot of things would've been straightened out.

—JIMI HENDRIX

I've had three wives and three guitars. I still play the guitars.

— ANDRES SEGOVIA

I destroyed a lot of guitars trying to get them to do what I wanted, but I learned something from every guitar I tore apart, and discovered even more things.

— EDDIE VAN HALEN

My dad is a huge rock and roll lead guitar fan. I didn't even really know that until recently.

— SLASH

Every guitarist…would tell me that I should have a flashy guitar…and I used to say, 'Why? Mine works, doesn't it? It's a piece of wood and six strings, and it works.

— ANGUS YOUNG

I'd think learning to play the guitar would be very confusing for sighted people.

— DOC WATSON

I don't want you to play me a riff that's going to impress Joe Satriani; give me a riff that makes a kid want to go out and buy a guitar and learn to play.

— OZZY OSBOURNE

We didn't have any instruments, so I had to use my guitar.

— MABELLE CARTER

That's all I wanted to do as a kid. Play a guitar properly and jump around. But too many people got in the way.

— SYD BARRETT

Guitar is easy, all it takes is 5 fingers, 6 strings and 1 a**hole.

— KEITH RICHARDS

Years from now, after I'm gone, someone will listen to what I've done and know I was here. They may not know or care who I was, but they'll hear my guitars speaking for me.

— CHET ATKINS

I am Rosa Parks with a Gibson guitar.

— TED NUGENT

I never wanted to sing. I just wanted to play rhythm guitar - hide in the back and just play.

— KURT COBAIN

Look what venison does to a goofy guitar player from Detroit? I'm going to be 54 this year and if I had any more energy I'd scare you.

— TED NUGENT

I want every girl in the world to pick up a guitar and start screaming.

— COURTNEY LOVE

I just want to be a guy with a guitar.

—JEFF BUCKLEY

I used to work in jobs I hated because I needed the money to buy a guitar. I know what it feels like to be depressed.

— CHRIS CORNELL

I can't even read notes. But I can teach someone how to make a guitar smoke.

— ACE FREHLEY

When I was growing up, there were two things that were unpopular in my house…one was me, and the other was my guitar.

– Bruce Springsteen

Recording is God's way of telling you
that you suck.

— BOB BROZMAN

I approach playing acoustic guitar more
of as a percussive instrument. It's fragile.
I don't have a lot of finesse when it
comes to my guitar playing.

— BILLIE JOE ARMSTRONG

There is no finer sonic-producing
weapon for a guitar slayer than a hand
crafter Gibson masterpiece.

— TED NUGENT

I'm the one that has to die when it's time for me to die, so let me live my life, the way I want to.

— JIMI HENDRIX

I've always been into guitars... we want to put keyboards on, but keyboard players don't look cool onstage…

— NOEL GALLAGHER

I'd like to have a beer-holder on my guitar like they have on boats.

— JAMES HETFIELD

The guitar is a wonderful instrument
which is understood by few.

– FRANZ SCHUBERT

The enthusiasm of the King toward
[this] music was such that the guitar
became the most fashionable
instrument…Everyone at court wanted
to learn, and God alone can imagine the
universal scraping and plucking that
ensued.

– MEMOIRS OF THE COUNT DE
GRAMMONT

Shut up and play your guitar.

– FRANK ZAPPA

I use heavy strings, tune low, play hard, and floor it. Floor it. That's technical talk.

— STEVIE RAY VAUGHAN

I remember one of the first gigs I played with that amp was at a local church…I dragged the amplifier down and started playing and everybody started yelling 'turn it down!'.

— ANGUS YOUNG

I wanted to be able to play guitar. I wanted to be able to make music hurt.

— ALEXIS KORNER

Why did they keep changing guitars and amplifiers when they were perfect? They did the same things with cars, if you ask me.

— BUDDY GUY

The Telecaster has two sounds - a good one and a bad one.

— JIMI HENDRIX

You know, once you've had that guitar up so loud on the stage, where you can lean back and volume will stop you from falling backward, that's a hard drug to kick.

— DAVID GILMOUR

[Commercial radio] is owned by one or two corporations now, and they're not in the music business…If you want to hear music, go buy a guitar.

— ELVIS COSTELLO

The disgusting stink of a too-loud electric guitar; now that's my idea of a good time.

— FRANK ZAPPA

At some point around '94 or '95, 'Rolling Stone' said that guitar rock was dead…that was the last issue of 'Rolling Stone' I ever bought.

— SCOTT IAN

I am the Great White Buffalo and I play an American-made Gibson guitar that can blow your head clean off at 100 paces.

— TED NUGENT

You're better off being a brick layer if you're going to play guitar than a sheet metal worker.

— ROGER DALTREY

From 1962 to 1965, the guitar became this icon of youth culture, thanks mostly to the Beatles.

— PAT METHENY

For me, I think the only danger is being too much in love with guitar playing…the guitar is only the instrument.

—JERRY GARCIA

Every once in a while I'll call up Eddie (Van Halen) and ask, Found that fourth chord yet.

— BILLY GIBBONS

Therefore you who rail at such that disturb your slumbers with unsuccessful and demoralizing attempts to subjugate a guitar, beware! For sooner or later your own time will come.

— MARK TWAIN

I still use the guitar pretty much just to hide my gut.

— GARTH BROOKS

Well I got this guitar and I learned how
to make it talk.

— BRUCE SPRINGSTEEN

The electric guitar was vital in helping
what I've achieved where would I be
without it? Playing awfully quietly, for a
start.

— KEITH RICHARDS

The world is full of amazing guitar
players, and you know it, and I know
it...it's a humbling experience...

— MARK KNOPFLER

I just fell down the stairs holding a guitar and accidentally wrote a One Direction song.

— WILL FERRELL

Too many amps, too much volume, it's just flat-out ear assault. Speedy guitars leave me not feeling detached but physically upset.

— JEFF BECK

I believe I love my guitar more than the others love theirs. For John and Paul…guitar playing is a means to an end.

— GEORGE HARRISON

The only thing I ever really wanted was a Strat ... I have a collection of more than 200 of them…

— YNGWIE MALMSTEEN

About ten years ago, I knew three chords on the guitar. Now, in 1982, I know three chords on the guitar.

— FREDDIE MERCURY

My guitar, I sing of thee 'Tis with thee that I decoy And ensnare enchantingly the ladies I enjoy.

— PIERRE DE RONSARD

I played the guitar for ten years before I
realized it wasn't a weapon.

— PETE TOWNSHEND

I play guitar my way; I've taken myself
to the edges of life my way; and I'm still
here....Whether or not I deserve to be is
another story.

— SLASH

I always thought the good thing about
the guitar was that they didn't teach it in
school.

—JIMMY PAGE

I've always wanted to smash a guitar over someone's head. You just can't do that with a piano.

— ELTON JOHN

And if I ever DO see [Kenny G] anywhere, at any function - he WILL get a piece of my mind, and maybe a guitar wrapped around his head.

— PAT METHENY

I just want to be able to play as fast as my brain goes, and my brain doesn't go all that fast.

— BRIAN MAY

Guitars are like women. You'll never get them totally right.

— SLASH

I keep guitars that are, you know, the neck's a little bit bent and it's a little bit out of tune. I want to work and battle it and conquer it…

— JACK WHITE

I smash guitars because I like them.

— PETE TOWNSHEND

All I have is this guitar, these chords and the truth.

—JON BON JOVI

Musically, I am still hooked and just hypnotized by the sound of the guitar itself. I mean, a guitar sounds good if you drop it on the floor.

— LOE KOTTKE

My mom thought the guitar was going to fizzle out in two weeks, that it was just a fad-and that was in 1958.

—JEFF BECK

We're just musically and rhythmically retarded. We play so hard that we can't tune our guitars fast enough.

— KURT COBAIN

If you wanna write a song, ask a guitar.

— NEIL YOUNG

He told me they didn't like the sound. Groups of guitars were on the way out.

— BRIAN EPSTEIN, BEATLES MANAGER, REGARDING A COMMENT BY DICK ROWE OF DECCA RECORDS

Players

GuitarQuotes

I started out playing guitar because Jimi Hendrix was my hero, so my roots were really based on …his style of playing.

—JOE SATRIANI

James Brown is the reason I play guitar.

— KEVIN EUBANKS

There are people these days who can do things on the guitar which are beyond my reach. There's one guy who plays with Queen who can do things I would dream of doing.

— ERIC CLAPTON

David Gilmour can do more with one note than most other guitar players can do with the whole fretboard.

— DAVE MUSTAINE

Chet Atkins... is probably the best guitar player who ever lived.

— CHARLEY PRIDE

…what really got me into guitar was watching a documentary about Jimi Hendrix and picking up the Woodstock soundtrack…I thought, 'I'm going to get a guitar.'

— KIRK HAMMETT

Pete Townshend used to crash chords and let the guitar feed back. He's overrated.

—RITCHIE BLACKMORE

Of the whole bunch of guys who play hollow body guitar, I think Herb Ellis has the most drive.

— LES PAUL

J.S. Bach was probably the most influential guy ever on me…All of a sudden I was thinking in all these other areas, instead of blues riffs."

— YNGWIE MALMSTEEN

For virtually every kid since 1968 who picked up a guitar to find his voice on the instrument, Jimmy Page has been the space that enables all our notes to be played.

—STEVE VAI

Nobody could understand why a guy would love his guitar, then all of a sudden turn around and try to destroy it. Jimi was just different.

— BOBBY WOMACK

And as far as guitars go, I loved Jimmy Bryant and Speedy West's stuff.

— WILLIE NELSON

Stevie Ray Vaughn…single handedly brought guitar and blues oriented music back to the marketplace.

– RICHARD BETTS

Every time I listen to Jeff Beck my whole view of guitar changes radically. He's way, way out, doing things you never expect.

—BRIAN MAY

... Andres Segovia literally created the genre of classical guitar, which hadn't existed before around 1910...

— ROGER McGUINN

The music of Hendrix wakes people up to their possibilities. It's more than just dreaming about being a guitar hero.

— CARLOS SANTANA

The invention of Bob Dylan with his guitar belongs in its way to the same kind of tradition…as the songs of Homer.

– ROBERT FITZGERALD

Buckethead [former Guns and Roses guitarist] is probably twice as good a guitar player as me and Slash combined…

– DAVE MUSTAINE

Barney Kessel is definitely the best guitar player in this world, or any other world.

– GEORGE HARRISON

... When it came time to hire a guitar player....Mike Bloomfield was the best guitar player I'd ever heard...

—BOB DYLAN

It's always funny to me when people use the phrase 'Best guitar player in the world'... But if I had to pick one, it would be Tommy Emmanuel.

— STEVE VAI

Thanks!

Thanks for taking the time to read these great quotes from guitar players. I hope you enjoyed them and were encouraged and inspired.

Would you take 30 seconds and review my book on Amazon? I would greatly appreciate it!

GuitarQuotes

Made in United States
North Haven, CT
15 December 2023

45775598R00075